THE BEST OF

You Might Be a Preacher If...

by Stan Toler
and Mark Hollingsworth

To our church families—Edmund First Church
of the Nazarene, Edmond, Oklahoma (Pastor Mark)
and Trinity Church of the Nazarene,
Oklahoma City, Oklahoma (Pastor Stan).

Thanks for the love and laughter we
experience each Sunday!

Introduction

It is with great joy that we present *The Best of You Might Be A Preacher If . . .* Your overwhelming response to Volume One and Two has made this laugh-a-page look at preacher's life possible. May these pages guide you into "ever-laughing" life!

You are loved!
Stan and Mark

Your wife plays the piano.

Your two car garage sometimes doubles as a Sunday School classroom.

You've ever waded in a creek wearing a neck-tie.

You've ever been tempted to stock the baptistry with catfish.

You've ever dreamed you were preaching only to awake and discover you were.

You've ever asked for the clergy discount at a garage sale.

You find yourself counting people at a sporting event.

You'd rather negotiate with a terrorist than the church organist.

You have a key ring that's bigger than the junior high school custodian's

You drive a buick
with over 100,000 miles on it.

You've ever wanted to wish people a "merry Christmas" at Easter 'cause that's the next time you'll see them.

You know the difference between a
pharmacist smock and a missionary shirt.

You've ever been tempted to put coupons in the local paper to compete with the Baptists.

Taking a nap on sunday afternoon is a spiritual experience.

You've ever been asked where to "plug in" the amplified Bible

You've ever been asked to do the invocation at a hog-callin' contest.

You've secretly wanted the worship team to drench you with "Gatorade" after a particularly good sermon.

You've ever been asked,
"So, what do you do the rest of the week?"

You read sermons to your kids at night instead of bedtime stories.

Your collar covers a multitude of chins.

You have a bumper sticker that says,
"if you love Jesus, don't honk . . . Tithe!"

You suffer weekly from P.M.S. (pre-message syndrome).

You've ever wanted to give the sound man a little "feedback" of your own.

Vacation Bible School is no vacation.

You have slides of the Holy Land.

You've ever had to explain that catechism is not a feline medical procedure.

You've ever had a personality conflict with a deacon you had one, and he didn't.

You've ever substituted Pennzoil for olive oil.

Wrist watch alarms go off while you're talking.

You overhear the head deacon praying "Lord, you keep him humble and we'll keep him poor."

You've wondered if there will be music directors in heaven.

People write grocery lists while you talk.

You only like two kinds of pie—hot or cold.

You often feel like you're herding mules rather than shepherding sheep.

You'd like to have a TV ministry but can't afford the wigs and makeup for your wife.

You've seen it all at weddings.

You've ever been asked to pray for a poodle.

if you've ever received an anonymous note.

Babies cry while you're talking.

You're sermons have a happy ending—
everybody's happy when it ends.

You've ever preached on television, but your wife made you get down before you broke something.

You've ever written a letter of resignation on Monday morning.

Instead of "pigging out" you "partake of nourishment."

You're job is never done.

You work like the devil for the Lord.

The words, "And in conclusion" mean absolutely nothing to you.

You get amused at people fussin' over the color of carpet.

You've ever wondered what the architect was thinking when he designed the baptismal robing room.

You exercise "religiously."

You wanted to tell your secretary who's the boss.

You've secretly wanted the head usher to give you a high-five after a particularly good sermon.

You're tired of being a shepherd and would rather be a cowboy and "brand" a few in your flock.

Running red lights in a funeral procession makes you feel important.

You use the word "holy" more times than Batman and Robin.

You've ever made up romantic songs to the tune of "How Great Thou Art."

You "will preach for food."

You wish Nike would make clerical clothing.

"Family night" is ever spent in a hospital lobby.

You hate beepers and cellular phones.

You have your own ideas about the "dead in christ."

You live in a glass house.

You thank the Lord everyday for caller ID.

You've ever wanted to tell Brother "know-it-all" a thing or two.

You've thought of developing a soundproof booth for people who cough in church.

You've ever wanted to try multilevel tithing.

You've ever suffered an anxiety attack while playing Bible Trivial Pursuit.

You've never said anything past twenty minutes that amounted to anything.

Your day-timer is the size of a family Bible.

You'd love to sleep in on Sundays.

You've ever been to a "bored" meeting.

People know you're "laying up treasures in heaven" by looking at your car.

You wish sister "talk-a-lot" would get caught in her own "mouthtrap."

You do the work of three men— Larry, Curley, and Moe.

You've ever had to explain that the epistles were not the wives of the apostles.

The only people who like change in your church are the wet babies.

Your kids are responsible for mowing the church yard.

You have an eye for fifteen-passenger vans.

You wish someone would steal some of your sheep.

You are lay-driven.

You have more bibles than the Gideons.

You're like a banana—every time you leave the bunch, you get "skinned."

People think you're an airport shuttle service.

You've seen more religion at a pool hall than you've seen at a church softball game.

You've anonymously telephoned your church's own dial-a-prayer line.

You own a "parsonal" computer.

You'd like to recruit some of Wal-Mart's greeters.

You've ever wanted to make French Fries out of some of your pew potatoes.

You're tired of people being "behind you 100 percent."

You know Hell's Angels are not just a motorcycle gang.

You could build a mansion with all
the "constructive" criticism you've received.

You've tried a little Miracle-Gro on your church.

You've ever received a phone call at 4:00 a.m. and the caller asks, "did I wake you?"

You can spot a church shopper through a stained glass window.

Every time you see a movie you get at least
five "new and inspired" sermon illustrations.

"Annual church Meeting" and "Armageddon" are one in the same to you.

People clip their fingernails while you talk.

You've ever been called a "holy roller" at a bowling alley.

You use the pray-as-you-go plan.

Your children have Biblical names.

Transients know you by name.

About the Authors

Stan Toler is a best-selling author, internationally known seminar leader, and pastor of Trinity Church of the Nazarene in Oklahoma City, Oklahoma.

stoler1107@aol.com • www.stantoler.com

Mark Hollingsworth is a humorist, inspirational speaker, author, and pastor of First Nazarene Church in Edmond, Oklahoma.

mhollingsworth24@sbcglobal.net • www.tolerbrotherstrio.com